DRUM EXERCISES
for the Pop, Funk, and R&B Player

**By Ralph Johnson
with Dan Gross**

Dedication
To my wife Susie and my two sons, John-Ralph and Mark-Anthony.
Three great reasons to be all you can be.
Thank you for your love and support.
–Ralph Johnson

All photos by Scott Mitchell

Recording Credits:
David Lewitt, Drums
Marshall Woodall, Engineer

Cherry Lane Music Company
Educational Director/Project Supervisor: Susan Poliniak
Director of Publications: Mark Phillips
Publications Coordinator: Rebecca Skidmore

ISBN 978-1-57560-828-0

Visit our website at www.cherrylaneprint.com

Contents

Foreword 3

About the Authors 3

Acknowledgments 5

Special Acknowledgment. 5

Maurice White Speaks of
Ralph Johnson 5

**Exercises for the Intermediate
Drummer**

Chapter 1 6
Exercises for the
Intermediate Drummer–
Technique

The Long Roll
Paradiddles
Rudimental Solos
    Slick
    High Tech
    Syncopod

Chapter 2 12
Exercises for the
Intermediate Drummer–
Sightreading

Triplets
Cut Time
    Gear Shifter
12/8 Time
    Duplicity

Chapter 3 27
Exercises for the
Intermediate Drummer–
Coordination

The Pretzel
Pretzel Variations

Chapter 4 30
Exercises for the
Advanced Drummer–
Technique

Two-Way Independence
Independence and Four-Way Coordination

Chapter 5 41
Exercises for the
Advanced Drummer–
Sightreading

Quarter Note Meters
Eighth Note Meters
Sixteenth Note Meters
Mixed Meters
    Meter Dance

Chapter 6 48
Exercises for the
Advanced Drummer–
Interpretation and Improvisation

Common Syncopated Big Band Rhythms
Drum Charts
    Something for Oliver
Samba Studies
    Off the Charts

Addendum 57

Foreword

In my now close to 40 years of recording and touring the world with Earth, Wind & Fire as their drummer/vocalist and percussionist, I've always been drawn toward the educational aspects of what I do. I came to learn that having a mentor to help you along with what you're trying to accomplish is priceless, so I, too, wanted to be a great teacher. Some of the greatest moments in my career have been those I've spent with my students, explaining various concepts and watching the light come on as they finally got it. This is not a book for those who are already out there and are well on their way to accomplishing their professional goals; it is rather for those who are still trying to get it together. For those of you who fit into this group, it's a written rhythmic barometer that will allow you to evaluate where you are in *your* world of rhythm in terms of its understanding and application.

Musically Yours,
Ralph Johnson, Ph.D.
Earth, Wind & Fire

About the Authors

RALPH JOHNSON

Ralph Johnson, an LA native born on July 4, 1951, grew up listening to a lot of music as a kid, but mainly jazz and the popular Motown sound. He remembers watching a local variety show, *The Johnny Otis Show*, and patting his hands together to various beats. His father bought him a pair of drumsticks and, soon after, a drum. More drums followed, and Ralph began to take drum lessons.

Ralph's family moved to Inglewood, California, where he graduated from Morningside High School in 1969. He remembers seeing the Forum being built, and envisioned playing there one day. If he only knew what the cards had in store for him, as a few short years later, his dream would indeed become a reality.

By 1968, Ralph had become involved with a local showcase called Maverick's Flat. He joined a local band called The Master's Children, with whom he vigorously played and honed his drumming skills.

One night, Maurice and Verdine White dropped by, checked out Ralph's performance, and were impressed. By late 1971, Ralph received a phone call to audition for Earth, Wind & Fire, and in 1972, he joined the legendary band as their drummer/percussionist/vocalist.

In 1972, Earth, Wind & Fire signed with Columbia Records and hit the music charts with their first single entitled "Mighty, Mighty." This was followed by the hits "Shining Star" and "Sun Goddess" (a Ramsey Lewis contribution).

In 1984, when Earth, Wind & Fire took a hiatus from the music industry, the group members began to pursue various projects. Ralph Johnson and Al McKay worked with Motown and produced the Temptations' hit single "Treat Her Like a Lady."

Earth, Wind & Fire regrouped in 1987 and hit the music charts with the single, "System of Survival." For seven years, the band toured and played many countries around the globe. By 1994, Maurice White decided that he would retire from touring with the band. He used his creative energy to form Magnet Visions, and works on in-house Earth, Wind & Fire collaborations and more studio productions.

With Maurice's blessing, the newly reformed band took to the road without their legendary leader. The fans embraced their arrival with great excitement and anticipation. The band has now incorporated a variety of other musicians into the show. After 38 years of performing with the group, Ralph can now be found on the front line, adding his own brand of slick choreography and percussive stylings.

Ralph's résumé reads like a who's-who of music royalty. Besides performing and recording with Earth, Wind & Fire, he has produced and performed with other artists on albums such as Howard Hewett's *If Only…* and *Christmas*, Audio Caviar's *Transoceanic*, and the Temptations' *Truly For You* and "Treat Her Like a Lady."

His songwriting prowess has been lauded by Jay-Z and Keyshia Cole, who each sampled his and Douglas Gibbs' "Sounds Like a Love Song." "Song Cry" is one of Jay-Z's most acclaimed songs, and "You've Changed" is featured on Keyshia's first album.

Currently, Ralph—along with the other two founding and continuing members of the band, Philip Bailey and Verdine White—is touring with Earth, Wind & Fire and working on Howard Hewett's upcoming release.

DAN GROSS

Since graduating Summa Cum Laude from Berklee College of Music in 1987, Dan Gross has toured, performed and recorded in a wide range of musical styles and venues in the U.S. and abroad. Equally at home in jazz clubs (Makoto Ozone), rock/funk/R&B concerts (Koutrakos, Lucy Lawless), and Broadway pits (*Grease!, Les Misérables, Chicago,* and *Rent*), Dan has drawn from this varied background for his work as a music educator and songwriter/composer. Recent writing projects include *Learn to Play Drums with Metallica: Volume 2* and a new original rock/pop musical, *Southern Rain*.

Acknowledgments

First, John Stix, thank you for being exceedingly patient while I finally got motivated. To you and your staff thank you. Rhonda Bedikian/Heavy Harmony Music: Thank you for your ongoing help and constantly reminding me of my deadlines. Thanks to the two great teachers I've had in my life, Clarence Johnston and Richard Wilson. You both did a great job. Finally, thanks to the two gentlemen I've had the pleasure of traveling the world with for the past 38 yrs—Philip Bailey and Verdine White. It just keeps getting better. God bless!

Special Acknowledgment

To Dan Gross, thank you for helping me to make this a very special project. Your creative input was a welcome addition and helped to round out the presentation.

Maurice White Speaks of Ralph Johnson

When speaking of individuals who are special, we ask the question: "What are the unique qualities that make him (or her) different?" We then start to observe him, and if the opportunity exists, we look over his shoulders and finally those qualities become clear.

Most of us are consciously trying to improve ourselves in one way or the other; through experiences we accomplish this. The knowledge we learn from each other, we store in our memory for future use, employing our own special qualities with it.

I found in Ralph some very special qualities. They are as follows: dedication, application, and practicality. These qualities I observed, and learned to appreciate, while creating music along with him. Ralph started playing music at the age of eight, learning his rudiments and fundamentals thoroughly and dedicating many long hours to practice daily. He joined the junior high and high school bands to get the proper direction and discipline in ensemble playing. Then, came the dance bands and, of course, the school talent shows, all the time building self-confidence with his goals and objectives clearly in focus. Ralph's experience and professionalism led him naturally to bigger and well-known names in music. The beginning of it all started with Johnny "Guitar" Watson, and from there he moved to the recording studios of L.A., working with a cavalcade of stars: Stanley Turrentine, Dee Dee Bridgewater, Deniece Williams, The Emotions, and, of course, Earth, Wind & Fire. Some of Ralph's major influences are "Philly" Joe Jones, Tony Williams, Roy Haynes, and Louie Bellson. In fact, his favorite is a double bass drum set.

In talking with Ralph casually, it is apparent to me that his goal, with the presentation of his book, is to motivate and prepare young drummers, through creative teaching, for a career in music. Being a drummer myself, I am truly motivated by this book's content. I sincerely hope it inspires you to find those unique qualities in yourself. Hats off to you, Ralph.

CHAPTER 1

Exercises for the Intermediate Drummer—Technique

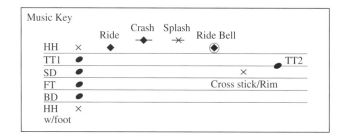

THE LONG ROLL

Long Roll Exercise 1

This first exercise is not simply an exercise—it is a *rudiment*, the first of twenty-six, and it's called the "long roll" or "momma-daddy."

I chose the long roll because when most drummers are asked to play it *open* (slow) or *closed* (fast), they tend to play the second note of each double stroke too weakly. By practicing the long roll with accents as in the example above, the player will soon achieve the desired sound—a roll that is smooth and even.

Long Roll Exercise 2

Here's another exercise that will, with a little practice, strengthen those double strokes and develop a seamless long roll. After you master it (don't forget the accents!), proceed to the paradiddle exercises.

PARADIDDLES

These paradiddle eighth note exercises are designed to improve your sound, touch, and speed. Begin by playing accents on the first note of each paradiddle in the first exercise; the accents are then shifted around in the second, third, and fourth. Be sure to maintain the same paradiddle sticking throughout.

R L R R L R L L R L R R L R L L

R L R R L R L L R L R R L R L L

R L R R L R L L R L R R L R L L

R L L R L R R L R L L R L R R L

Practice the following 16th note exercise while again maintaining the proper paradiddle sticking (RLRRLRLL) throughout and paying close attention to the accents. Try starting the exercise with the left hand as well.

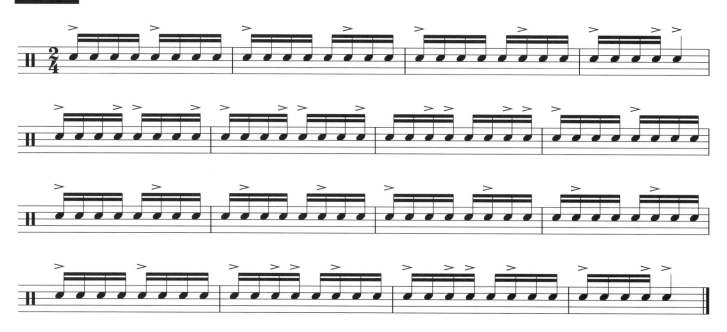

Once you have mastered that on the snare drum, try "orchestrating" it by playing all of the accents on the toms (right-hand accents on the floor tom and left-hand accents on the high tom). The first line, for example, would be played as follows.

R L R R L R L L   R L R R L R L L   R L R R L R L L   R L R R L

Finally, add the hi-hat (left foot) on the "and" of each beat. The second line would look like this.

R L R R L R L L   R L R R L R L L   R L R R L R L L   R L R R L R L L

RUDIMENTAL SOLOS

These rudimental solos have a great feel and groove, and present a challenging combination of rolls, flams, and ruffs. Following each solo are a few helpful hints for the tricky bits.

SLICK

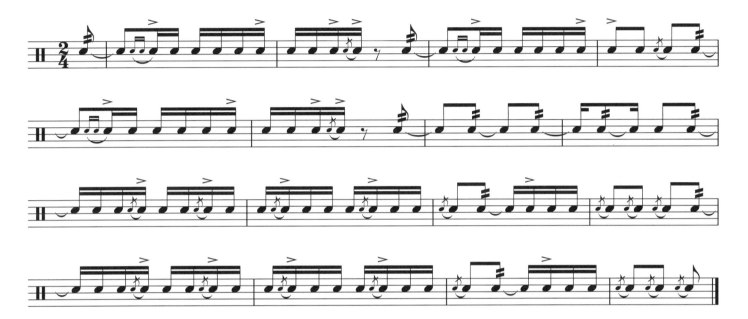

- Pick-up bar: The five-stroke roll is a pick-up beginning on the "and" of beat 2.

- Measures 2, 4, 6: The ruffs are played as a pair of soft double-stroke grace notes followed by a stronger single "principal note" (LLR or RRL).

- Measure 8: Both of the rolls in bar 8 are five-stroke rolls. The one in the first beat starts on the "e" of that beat and is played with double strokes on the "e" of 1 and the "and" of 1, followed by a single stroke on the "a" of 1.

- Reminder: Don't forget to play all of the accented notes just a touch stronger than the rest so that they pop out a little for the listener.

- Measures 4, 8, 16: The proper sticking for the flamacue (another of the standard 26 rudiments) is LRLRLLR or RLRLRRL, with the accent on the second 16th note.

- Measure 7: This bar can be played as another rudiment, the flam tap, by using the sticking LRRRLLLR or RLLLRRRL.

- Measures 9, 10, 13: These are played as 13-stroke rolls beginning on the "and" of beat 1 and ending on the downbeat of the next bar.

- Measure 12: The sextuplet is simply an alternative notation for two consecutive 16th note triplets. In this case, the rhythm would be counted "1–trip-let–and–trip-let."

SYNCOPOD

- Measure 6: The first beat shows a 16th note triplet followed by two 16th notes and is counted "1–trip–let–and–a."

- Measures 9–14: The real challenge here is in counting the rests properly and leaving the appropriate amount of space between the notes. If you were to play something like this in a band setting, these rhythmic punctuations would be referred to collectively as *stop time*. The "air," or breaks between notes, could leave room for a vocalist's lyrics, an instrumental soloist (guitar, saxophone, etc.), or just some silence, which can be very effective musically.

- For a further application, try playing "Slick," "High Tech," and "Syncopod" on the snare drum while simultaneously playing one of the following patterns in the feet.

CHAPTER 2

Exercises for the Intermediate Drummer—Sightreading

While not every musical situation requires the ability to *sightread* (to read and play written music on the spot), a reasonable level of proficiency in this area can be very useful. It can come in quite handy in both live performance and recording situations, and it can also be an excellent self-teaching tool.

Beyond the basic note values and time signatures, there are a number of written rhythms that, while not uncommon, can be very tricky. I'll cover a few now and more later.

TRIPLETS

Eighth Note Triplets

Starting with the eighth note triplet, play the example below while counting "1–and–a, 2–and–a, 3–and–a, 4–and–a" as indicated to lock in the proper feel. As you know, when playing "regular" eighth notes, you are placing two notes evenly within the space of one beat. With eighth note triplets, you are squeezing three notes evenly into that same one-beat space.

TRACK 13

Eighth Note Triplets with Rests

Now, try these eighth note triplets with rests. Your counting should remain the same throughout ("1–and–a, 2–and–a, 3–and–a, 4–and–a") whether counting notes or rests.

TRACK 14

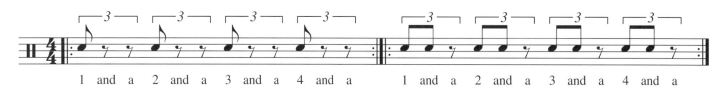

Eighth Note Triplets (Alternate Notation)

The first five patterns in the example above can also be written using quarter triplet notes or rests as follows.

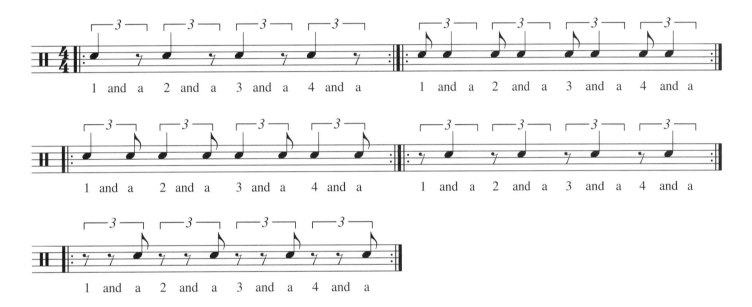

Quarter Note Triplets

Quarter note triplets are played as if omitting every other eighth triplet note; continue counting eighth triplets as before. Play and count these quarter note triplets enough to "internalize" them, so you can feel the pulse of the triplet instinctively.

TRACK 15

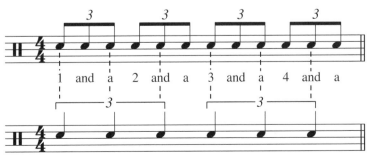

Half Note Triplets

Here we have the elusive half note triplet!

The half note triplet is *elusive* because if it's not played just right, it turns out sounding like something else. The important concept of this exercise lies in the counting and playing of the half note triplets in a *very* slow 4/4 meter.

TRACK 16

I've found that no matter what the pattern is, if you can *count* it, you can *play* it! And, if you practice *slowly*, you'll practice *accurately*.

Half Note Triplets Subdivided

Now, look at the example below. When you're playing the half note triplet, if you mentally count eighth note triplets while playing only the beats that are indicated for the half notes, then you'll have it!

TRACK 17

Compound Triplets

In this next example, we'll explore compound triplets—a layering of triplets within triplets, if you will. After the "run-of-the-mill" eighth note triplets in the first line and "standard fare" quarter note triplets in the second line, the third line indicates that an eighth note triplet is to be played in the space of each quarter triplet note.

Because these "triplets within triplets" are played faster than the straight-up eighth note triplets with which we began this chapter, we do not count them using the same "1–and–a, etc." syllables. In fact, there is no formalized way to count them, but if you can naturally feel the pulse of the quarter note triplets first—and then fit eighth note triplets into each of those pulses—then you're home free!

It's a little tricky, but it's a great mental musical exercise. And getting "inside" the beats this way will give you a better understanding for time and space within the musical grooves presented later in this text.

In the fourth line, you'll play a set of four 16th notes in place of each quarter triplet note. Again, as there is no formal counting system, simply lock in to the quarter note triplet pulse and fit the 16ths evenly.

The fifth and final line of the example simply shows another (and more commonly used) way to notate those "16ths within quarter note triplets," this time written as six-note groupings or *sextuplets*.

Now, it's time to put this new knowledge to use in some triplet exercises. Remember to subdivide and count those eighth note triplets throughout.

Triplet Exercise 1

This exercise contains nothing that you haven't encountered already. Refer to the previous examples if necessary. Listen to and play along with the recordings of these exercises on the accompanying CD to be sure that you are reading and counting these rhythms accurately.

TRACK 19

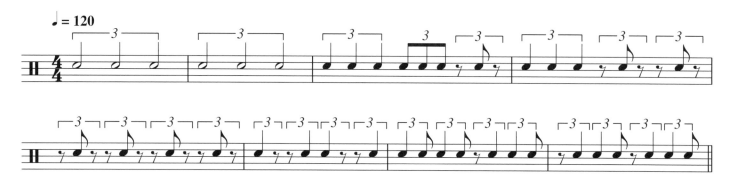

Triplet Exercise 2

This exercise is similar to the previous one, but with the addition of a few ties. *Ties* are curved lines that connect two notes together. A tie indicates that you simply play the first note (the one before, or to the left of, the tie) and count through but do *not* play the second note (the one after, or to the right of, the tie). In the seventh measure, for example, you would play every note except those that fall squarely on beats 2, 3, and 4.

TRACK 20

Triplet Exercise 3

This one takes things a step further, applying some ties to quarter note triplets as well. Again, count all of the subdivisions (eighth note triplets), and do not play any notes to the immediate right of the ties.

TRACK 21

Triplet Exercise 4

And now for the tough ones—the compound triplets! Take your time, keep the tempo slow, and don't give up. If you get stuck, there are some measure-by-measure hints on the next page to help you figure this one out.

TRACK 22

- Measure 1: Rhythmically, these are plain old eighth note triplets. The accents actually delineate or "spell out" half note triplets.

- Measure 2: As written, this measure indicates three four-note groupings of eighth notes under a half note triplet bracket. The accents again delineate the rhythm of a half note triplet. In actuality, this is just another way to notate the rhythm in measure 1. The two measures are written differently but are played (and should sound) exactly the same.

- Measure 3: These four-note groupings of 16th notes under the half note triplet bracket are played exactly twice as fast as the eighth note groupings in measure 2. Another way to look at it is that the accents delineate quarter note triplets. If you can feel the quarter note triplet pulse and place the four-note groupings accordingly, then you've got it.

- Measure 4: The accents in measure 3 clearly set the quarter note triplet pulse. The key to playing measure 4 accurately is to "flip the switch" from feeling quarter notes (four to the measure) as the central beat or pulse to feeling the quarter note triplets instead as the beat/pulse. Using that new quarter triplet pulse (six pulses to the measure) as a guide, the first triplet in measure 4 starts on the first "beat" and ends with an accented quarter note on the second. Likewise, the next triplet begins on the third of these "beats" and ends with another accented quarter note on the fourth. Finally, the last one begins on the fifth "beat" and ends with a quarter note on the sixth.

- Measures 5 through 8: Again, beginning with measure 4, the trick here is to feel as the pulse (i.e., tap your foot to) the quarter note triplets starting in measure 4. You can begin making that switch in measure 3 as the accents clearly state that quarter note triplet pulse. Continue to tap your foot and feel this as your new six-beats-to-the-bar pulse for measures 5 through 8 as well.

CUT TIME

"What is it that looks like 4/4 time, but sounds like 2/4?"

Cut time!

"And what is cut time?"

Actually, cut time (2/2) is 4/4 time that has been devalued by 50%. A whole note that normally receives four beats in 4/4 time receives two beats in cut time. A half note that receives two beats in 4/4 time receives one beat in cut time, and so on.

To help you understand what cut time looks and sounds like, the patterns below are written in cut time, while the patterns directly across from them are written in 2/4. A study of these patterns will be time well spent (with no devaluation).

Rhythm Patterns in Cut Time and 2/4

Written   **Played**

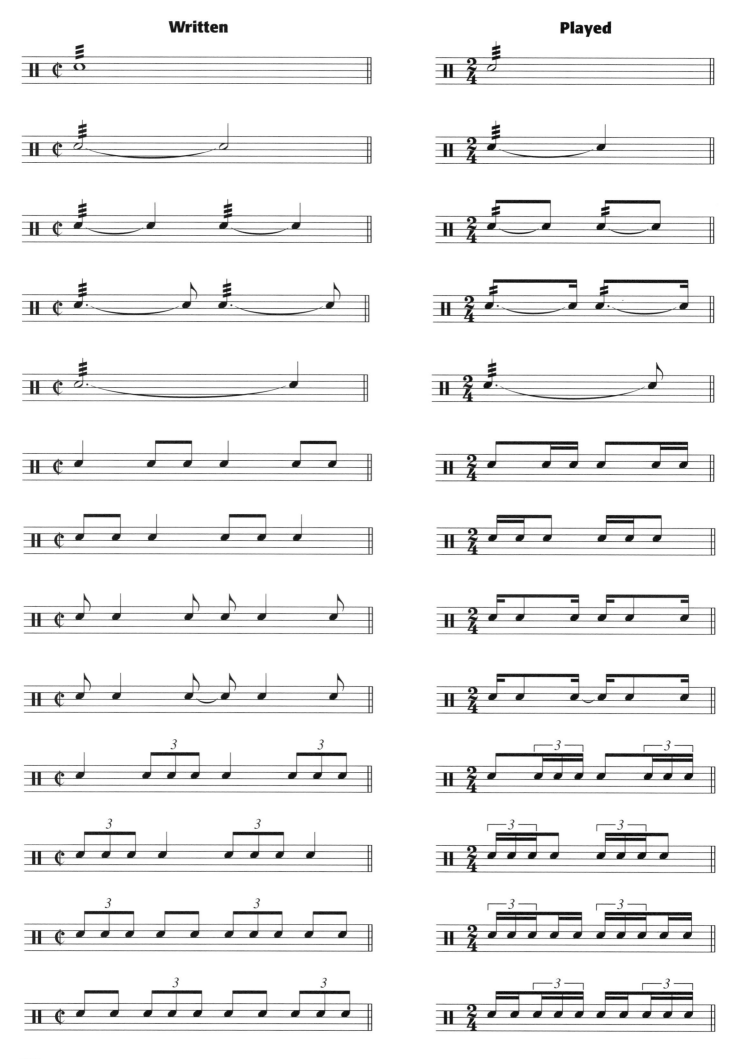

Rolls in Cut Time

Here are some fun and challenging exercises written in cut time. These rolls should be played as five-stroke rolls. The first one begins on beat 1 and ends on the "and" of beat 1 while the second roll begins on beat 2 and ends on the "and" of 2. The half note rolls should be played as nine-stroke rolls, and the dotted half note rolls as 13-stroke rolls. The dotted quarter note rolls should be played as seven-stroke rolls. Refer as necessary to the examples above that compare cut time to 2/4 time to double-check your counting.

TRACK 23

Triplets in Cut Time

This next exercise focuses more on cut time triplets. Feeling the music in two, the quarter note triplets will play like the eighth note triplets you're familiar with in 4/4 or 2/4 time, and the cut time eighth note triplets will play like 16th note triplets in 4/4 or 2/4. Again, just sneak a peek back at the previous counting examples as needed. It's always better to try to get it right the first time!

TRACK 24

Sixteenth Notes in Cut Time

Now, let's get those wrists, fingers, and sticks cranking with a bunch of cut time 16ths which, as you can probably guess by now, will feel and be played like 32nd notes from 4/4 time.

GEAR SHIFTER

The following solo should lock in the concept of cut time and its relationship to 4/4. "Gear Shifter" features a variety of triplet figures and syncopated, offbeat rhythms, but it gets its name from the fact that it bounces back and forth between 4/4 and cut time. The notation at measure 5 indicates that the quarter note pulse in the 4/4 section becomes the half note pulse in the cut time section. In other words, the speed of the 4/4 (common time) quarter note equals that of the cut time half note. The second line may appear the same as the first, but it should sound twice as fast. At measure 9, we have the opposite marking. The half note cut time pulse will revert and become the quarter note pulse in 4/4 once again, thereby effectively cutting the speed of the music in half.

Remember, too, that the rolls will change from 4/4 to cut time. For example, the dotted quarter note 13-stroke rolls in measure 9 (4/4) become seven-stroke rolls in measure 13 (cut time).

As always, practice slowly at first, taking care that your counting is accurate before pushing the tempo.

12/8 TIME

This time signature can look a little intimidating, but 12/8 simply indicates that there are 12 eighth notes per measure. 12/8 time typically has a swaying feel with four main pulses, or beats, with a grouping of three eighth notes in each. Each of those four beats could be represented by a single dotted quarter note.

12/8 Eighths = 4/4 Eighth Triplets

In other words, 12/8 time feels as though there is an emphasis on the first, fourth, seventh and tenth eighth notes in the measure as follows: "**1**–2–3, **4**–5–6, **7**–8–9, **10**–11–12." Though technically correct, counting up to 12 is a bit cumbersome; therefore, it is common to count the eighth notes in 12/8 like this: "**1**–and–a, **2**–and–a, **3**–and–a, **4**–and–a." As you can see below, eighth notes in 12/8 time can also be written as eighth note triplets in 4/4.

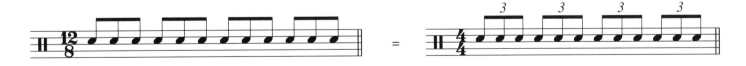

Rhythm Patterns in 12/8

Count and play through the following examples to get acquainted with some common 12/8 rhythms.

Rolls in 12/8

Rolls in 12/8 are typically played as follows:

Eighth Note Rolls	=	Five-Stroke Rolls
Dotted Eighth Note Rolls	=	Seven-Stroke Rolls
Quarter Note Rolls	=	Nine-Stroke Rolls
Dotted Quarter Note Rolls	=	13-Stroke Rolls

The 12/8 time signature has a very satisfying "swaying" feel once you become comfortable with it. Try the following exercises and solo with that in mind.

Duple, Triple, and Compound Meters

TRACK 29

Well, here you are playing snare drum with the Los Angeles Philharmonic, and it's opening night at the Hollywood Bowl. The overture is a piece written in 6/8, and the first two measures look exactly like the ones in the example above. When you reach the measure with the bracketed eighth notes, do you:

1. Switch to bass drum?
2. Tacet?
3. Roll?
4. None of the above?

Basically, there are two types of meters: *duple meters*, which have a down-up feeling and are counted "1–and–2–and, etc.," and *triple meters*, which have a triplet feeling and are counted "1–2–3, 4–5–6," etc. There's also a combination of the two, or *compound meter*, where sets of two are played over a "three" feel, as in the second measure in the example above.

Compound Meter Exercise

Here's an exercise that should give you a better understanding of this compound meter idea.

TRACK 30

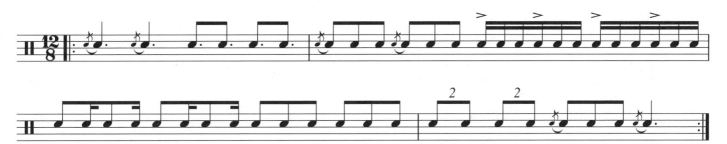

DUPLICITY

Now, let's explore this concept further by looking at a 12/8 (triple meter) solo, but this time utilizing what I call a "compound duple" sound. While 12/8 music is written and felt in groups of three, accents can be used to imply polyrhythms and create phrases in two-note groupings (as in measures 1, 4, 6, 10, 11, and 14) or four-note groupings (as in measures 3, 8, 9, 15, and 16). Refer back to the earlier examples and exercises if any of the rhythms are unclear.

TRACK 31

Now that you have some serious stick control and sight-reading chops together, take a seat at the kit and dive into the next chapter.

CHAPTER 3

Exercises for the Intermediate Drummer—Coordination

THE PRETZEL

So much of drumming is about developing complete or near-complete control over what the different limbs are doing. There are infinite ways to approach this and countless exercises to practice. Here's one that's guaranteed to tie you up in knots for a while!

The Pretzel

I call this little gem of an exercise "The Pretzel." Your hands play doubles while your feet play paradiddles. Think about that! Better yet, don't think about it—just try it!

TRACK 32

The Pretzel with 16ths

Give this one a shot—same idea, but the hands are playing 16th notes.

TRACK 33

PRETZEL VARIATIONS

Now, try "flipping" the parts. Play the paradiddles in your hands and the double strokes in your feet!

Pretzel Variation 1

Pretzel Variation 2

Pretzel Variations 3–6

Now, try those four exercises starting with the left hand and left foot as shown below.

If you really want to torture yourself, try the exercises starting with the opposite hand and foot. In other words, start with the right hand and left foot, or with the left hand and right foot. Experiment and come up with your own "Pretzel" variations, and write them down in the empty staves provided. These make great warm-up exercises before practice sessions, rehearsals, and performances.

CHAPTER 4

Exercises for the Advanced Drummer–Technique

TRACK 34

TWO-WAY INDEPENDENCE

This exercise serves as an introduction to *independence*, which, from a technical standpoint, is the very essence of jazz drumming. I've found that most students, when confronted with this exercise, have a tendency to play the eighth notes as if they were dotted eighths and 16ths—a different sound altogether from what is intended!

The key to playing this exercise is as follows.

TRACK 35

Use your left hand to play the eighth notes, and your right hand to play the grace notes and the 16ths that lead into beats 1 and 3, and you'll have it!

Now, take a look at the two-bar combinations that begin by utilizing eighth notes in the left hand, and then progress to dotted eighths and 16ths. Remember to play the hi-hat on beats 2 and 4 while playing the bass drum on beats 1 *through* 4 like this.

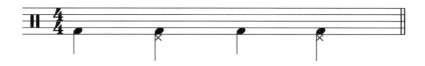

Practice all of the following two-bar hand pattern combinations in the same manner with the hi-hat on 2 and 4 and the bass drum on 1, 2, 3, and 4. If you have any difficulty at first, try leaving out the feet until you are completely comfortable with the hands alone. Then, add the feet again.

TRACK 41

TRACK 42

TRACK 43

Once you have mastered the two-bar combinations, put it all together with these two 16-bar solos.

TRACK 44

TRACK 45

In this next section, the left hand plays dotted eighth and 16th note patterns. Continue to play the hi-hat on 2 and 4 and the bass drum on all four beats. As before, if a particular exercise gives you any difficulty, break it down and learn the hands parts first. Add the feet—one at a time, if necessary—when you are ready.

TRACK 46

TRACK 47

TRACK 48

For the following 16-bar solos, continue to play the hi-hat and bass drum as before.

INDEPENDENCE AND FOUR-WAY COORDINATION

The study of independence continues with the incorporation of hand and foot combinations against the ride cymbal and hi-hat. As you'll soon see, this also turns out to be a study in coordination. In the exercise above and the ones that follow, the bass drum should be played wherever there is an eighth rest in the snare part. In other words, the bass drum fills in the spaces between the snare drum notes to create a flowing dialogue of eighth note triplets between the left hand and right foot.

These hand and foot combinations represent some of the patterns played by the jazz greats Art Blakey, Max Roach, Elvin Jones, Roy Haynes, Billy Hart, Tony Williams, and "Philly" Joe Jones, to name but a few. These pioneers of jazz drumming have had, through their various styles, tremendous influence on drummers such as Jack DeJohnette, Lenny White, Billy Cobham, Leon Ndugu Chancler, Steve Gadd, Jeff Watts, Adam Nussbaum, Marvin "Smitty" Smith, Steve Smith, and countless others.

Practice each exercise until it flows without sounding mechanical. One of the best things you can do to achieve a relaxed, natural feel is to listen to recordings by the drummers mentioned above.

Important: Remember to play the hi-hat (left foot) on beats 2 and 4 throughout. This will serve as your time-keeping "anchor."

TRACK 59

TRACK 60

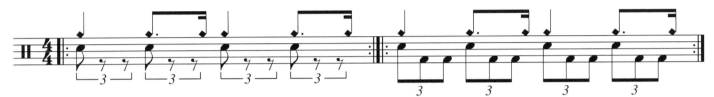

TRACK 61

TRACK 62

TRACK 63

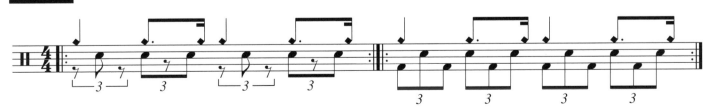

For the remainder of the exercises in this chapter, only the ride cymbal and snare drum parts have been written out. Continue to play the bass drum wherever eighth rests occur in the snare part, and don't forget the hi-hat on beats 2 and 4. At times, you may find it necessary (and advisable) to break a pattern down like this.

1. Learn the ride cymbal/snare drum parts first to create "two-way independence."
2. Add the bass drum to create "three-way independence."
3. Add the hi-hat "anchor" when "three-way independence" is comfortable and solid.

Two-Bar Combinations

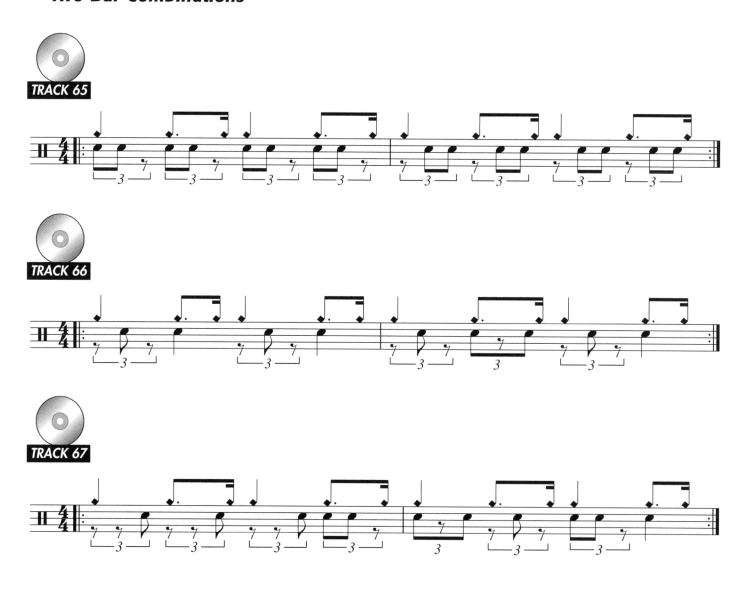

TRACK 68

TRACK 69

TRACK 70

TRACK 71

TRACK 72

Sixteen-Bar Solo

CHAPTER 5

Exercises for the Advanced Drummer—Sightreading

During my years as a student of drums and percussion, I've found the study of odd time signatures to be the most interesting and fun. It's the kind of study that never becomes boring because of the infinite combinations of rhythms.

The odd-time exercises that follow have been divided into three groups: quarter note, eighth note, and 16th note meters. The beat in each of these meters remains constant, as indicated by one of the following.

You should also recognize that subdivisions may occur in meters that have five, seven, or nine beats per measure. For instance, a piece that is written in 5/8 could be "in five," meaning it is phrased as five equal beats per measure, or it could be subdivided and phrased as a 2/8 + 3/8 or 3/8 + 2/8 measure.

QUARTER NOTE METERS

In these meters, the note values and counting are similar to what you are used to in 4/4. The only difference is the number of beats per measure.

Here's an exercise in 3/4, 5/4, and 7/4.

EIGHTH NOTE METERS

For time signatures in which "8" is the denominator (lower number), each eighth note receives one beat or pulse. In these meters, count/tap/feel the eighth notes as you would quarter notes in 3/4, 5/4, 7/4, etc.

SIXTEENTH NOTE METERS

Though it might be hard to imagine, in these meters each 16th note receives one beat/count. For example, the first measure below would be counted "1–2–3," and the second measure (with the 32nd notes) would actually be counted "1–and–2–3–and."

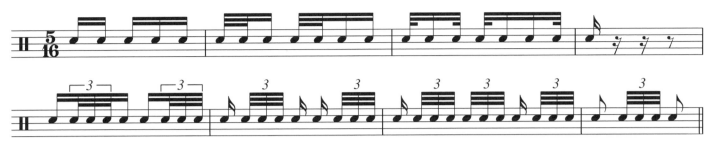

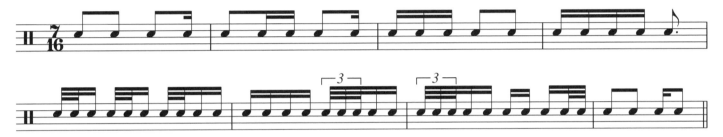

Here's an exercise using 3/16, 5/16, and 7/16 meters. Good luck!

MIXED METERS

Take your time with the following mixed odd-meter solo, and stick with it. With a little patience and attention to detail, you will get it! Accuracy is far more important than sheer speed, so focus on counting and playing all of the rhythms properly. Try working through it. If you need a little help, there are some tips on the next page.

METER DANCE

TRACK 86

One trick to figuring out a piece like this that switches constantly between meters is to subdivide and feel all of the 16th notes (the lowest common denominator) throughout the shifting meters. The speed of the 16th notes should remain constant. For example, if the first line of the solo were written with nothing but 16th notes, it would look like this.

1 and 2 and 3 and   1 2 3   1 e and a 2 e and a 3 e and a   1 and 2 and 3 and 4 and 5 and

There would be six 16th notes in the first measure, three in the second, 12 in the third, and ten in the fourth; you could count them as indicated. All other note values, relative to the 16th note, would be the same as you are accustomed to. An eighth note still equals two 16ths, a quarter note equals four, etc. Therefore, the first line of the solo as it is actually written can be counted like this.

1   2   3   1   2   3   1   2   3   and   1   2   3   4   and   5

CHAPTER 6

Exercises for the Advanced Drummer–Interpretation and Improvisation

This advanced study deals with interpreting and improvising around syncopated big band figures. The interesting thing about playing big band music is that while the drummer is playing the syncopated figures—which are usually horn section "punches"—that person must also *fill*, and the fills are what give big bands such an exciting sound.

Most big band drum music provides only a basic guide as to what to play, often spelling out just the key rhythms played by the rest of the band. It is the drummer's job, then, to interpret and create on the spot ("improvise") his or her part based on the limited information written into the music.

The following exercises can help you to understand how to fill out a rhythm written in your drum music. Before you begin, though, there's a very important point to be covered, the *touchdown point*. In reading syncopation figures that end on an upbeat, knowing on which downbeat to touchdown is very important. The downbeat immediately following the upbeat at the end of the figure being played will go by too fast to be counted, so you count and touchdown (land) on the next available downbeat. In the examples below, each touchdown point is indicated by a circle.

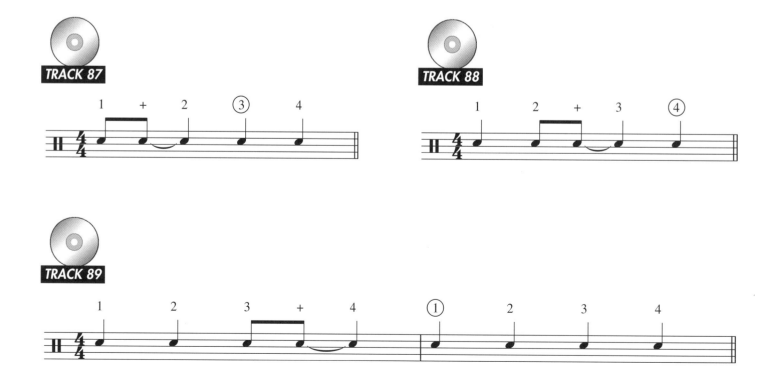

COMMON SYNCOPATED BIG BAND RHYTHMS

Now, take a look at some common rhythms—as written and with possible fills—that you may encounter when playing. Notice the interplay between the snare drum and the bass drum in the fills that colors and supports the band figures.

Written   **Played**

DRUM CHARTS

Below is an example of a typical big band drumset part or *drum chart*. As you can see, it is really just a basic roadmap that leaves quite a bit up to the taste, skill, and discretion of the player. To help you to decipher the chart and decide what to play, refer to the guidelines following the music.

SOMETHING FOR OLIVER

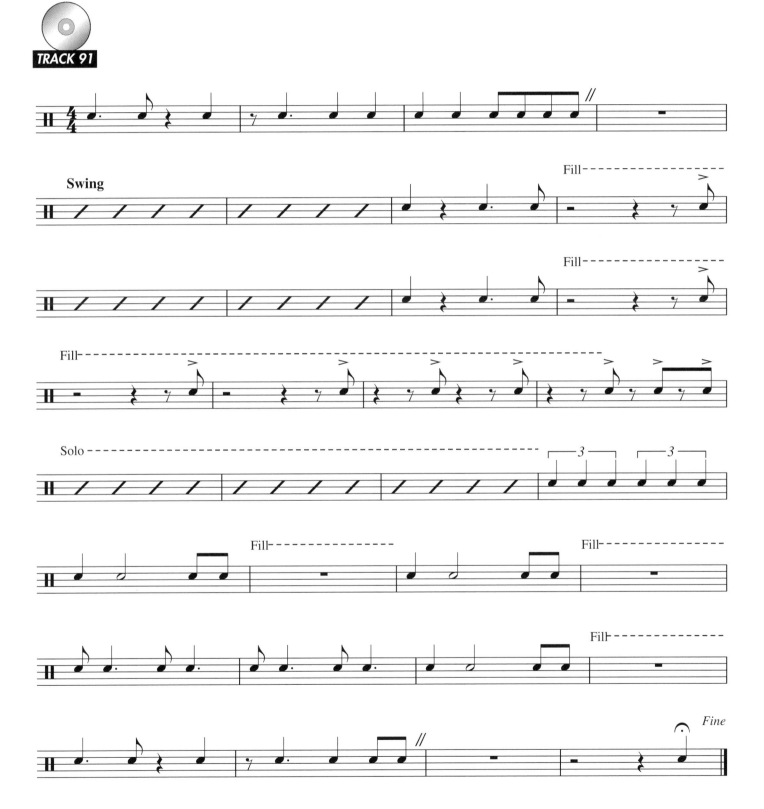

Drum Chart Interpretation Guidelines

Written Figures

When specific rhythms are given (as in the first three measures of "Chart House"), imagine a horn section phrasing those figures with you, and play the written rhythms while filling in and around them.

Slashes

When there is nothing but a few slashes and a style indication (as in the first two measures of the second system), just play "time." In this instance, the drummer is being told to lay down a swing groove to accompany and support the music. Something like this might work.

Fill

The "Fill" marking indicates that the drummer should play a short musical idea in the space shown to set up the written rhythms to follow. For example, measure 8 might be played like this.

Solo

At the section marked "Solo" in system 5, it is your moment to switch from supporting and accompanying the rest of the band to shining in the spotlight. This is your drum solo, and you are free to play whatever you deem suitable—as simple and subtle or as complicated and flashy as you want to make it. The most important thing is that you stay in time. Get creative and have fun, but don't rush, drag, or drop any beats.

Coming Out of the Solo

At the end chf this solo, there are rhythms (a pair of quarter note triplets) that are figures you must play with the band to bring them back in. Whatever you play in your solo, try to make things rhythmically clear so that the band can nail those figures precisely with you.

Fermata

The *fermata,* or "bird's eye," marking over the final quarter note in the last measure indicates that this last note is held out until it's cut off by the bandleader. The drummer has the option here of just letting his or her final note (a cymbal, perhaps) ring out, or he could, for instance, play a long snare or cymbal roll. There is always the "hit everything including the kitchen sink" approach—whatever works for you and makes musical sense!

As you can see, the great thing about the way in which most big band drum music is written is the amount of freedom the drummer has to decide exactly what and how much (or little) to play. Using the chart as an outline, the drummer is encouraged to use his or her ears to listen to what the rest of the band is playing and to create an appropriate, unique, and personal drum part using his taste and skill level as guides.

The challenge that comes with having that kind of musical freedom to improvise one's part is that the drummer must develop the ability to read what is printed on the page and instantly interpret it, deciding when to fill, when to solo, when to accent or support the band's parts, and when to play just the accompanying role of timekeeper. Experiment and try many different approaches. Listen as much as you can to live performances and recordings of drummers who play in this style. Your developing musical sense, experience, and knowledge will steer you in the right direction.

SAMBA STUDIES

The purpose of this exercise is to develop a solid foot foundation for the samba, a South American rhythm that, in my opinion, is often overlooked by young aspiring drummers. It's a rhythm that you'll find used a great deal in contemporary music. This exercise should be practiced daily at various tempos and with varied dynamics—that is, slow to fast, loud to soft.

Once you've mastered this foot portion of the samba and you're dancing on your pedals, move up top and add the hands. Remember that in order for the samba to sound good, the feet must be solid and consistent. Here are some ideas to try over the samba foot pattern.

Play the right and left hands together ("in unison") on the hi-hat and snare.

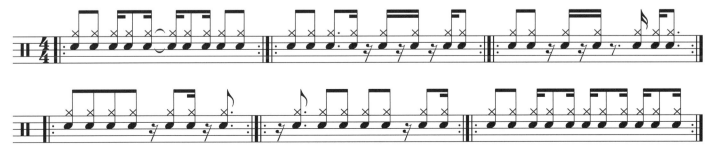

This variation utilizes the sound of the left stick on the rim, while the right hand plays eighth notes on a closed hi-hat.

TRACK 96

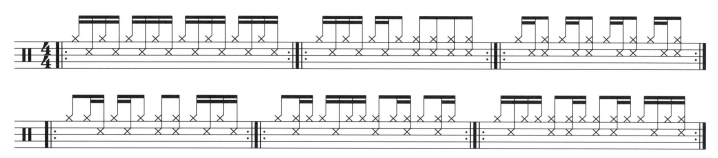

In this last rhythm, the right stick plays on the bell of the ride cymbal, while the left hand is split between the high tom and the low (floor) tom.

TRACK 97

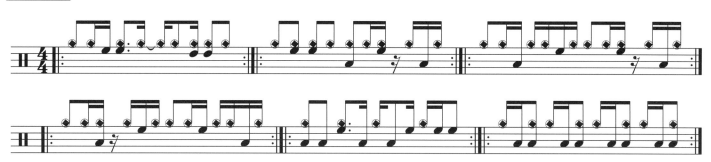

Once you familiarize yourself with these patterns, try creating your own samba variations. Hear a pattern in your head, and then sit down at the kit and work out the coordination. If it helps you to write your ideas down, use the following empty staves to transcribe your favorite original samba grooves.

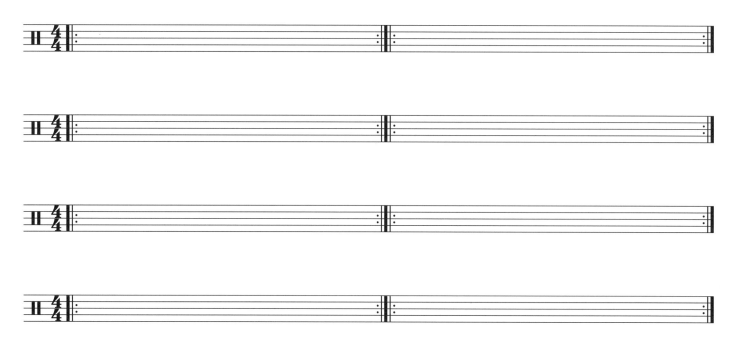

OFF THE CHARTS

Now, use a favorite samba pattern to read, interpret, and play the following chart. Practice various fills to "set up" the written rhythmic figures.

TRACK 98

Intro (Introduction)

The composer has written out a very specific part for the drummer. Your first approach should be to honor and play exactly what is written. It is common and accepted practice for drummers to have some leeway in straying from "the ink," but one should always begin with the intended part when specified.

A Section

The "(ens.)" figures in the fourth bar are *ensemble*, or full band rhythms. The drummer could just play samba time in the first two beats of the measure or lead into the figures with a clear "set-up" fill.

B Section

The articulation markings in the seventh and eighth bars of this section indicate the band's phrasing. A note with a "–" (called a *tenuto* marking) is played just a little longer than written. One with a "." it is played *staccato*, or short.

C and D Sections

The drummer should fill and solo around the written figures in these sections. For example, in the last bar of section C, you should play the accented quarter notes, but you are free to fill in a bit between those quarters.

D.S. al Fine

This marking in the last measure indicates that, after the final bar, the chart goes back to the sign at the beginning of section A and continues until the "Fine" marking in the last measure of that section.

Addendum

What follows is a partial list of books that I've either played through and use in my teaching, or are a part of my personal library.

1. *W. F. Ludwig Drum Instructor* by Ludwig Drum Company
2. *N.A.R.D. Rudimental Solos* by Ludwig Drum Company
3. *Syncopation* by Ted Reed
4. *Advanced Techniques for the Modern Drummer* by Jim Chapin
5. *Portraits in Rhythm* by Anthony J. Cirone
6. *Cut Time* by Sam Ulano
7. *Odd Time Reading Text* by Louis Bellson and Gil Breines
8. *Podemski's Standard Snare Drum Method* by Benjamin Podemski
9. *Modern Rudimental Swing Solos* by Charles Wilcoxon
10. *Contemporary Snare Drum Studies* by Fred Albright
11. *Control of the Drum Set—Phrasing for the Soloist* by Alexander Lepak
12. *Brushworks: The New Language for Playing Brushes* by Clayton Cameron
13. *Rudimental Snare Drum Grooves* by Johnny Lee Lane and Richard L. Walker Jr.
14. *Rick's Licks* by Rick Gratton
15. *Inside, Outside* by Billy Moore
16. *Stick Control* by George Lawrence Stone
17. *Modern Method* by Carl E. Gardner
18. *Future Sounds* by David Garibaldi

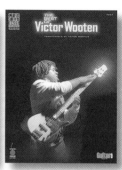

Great DVD selections from CHERRY LANE

MORE HOT DRUM BOOKS AND DVDs FROM CHERRY LANE

STEVEN ADLER'S GETTING STARTED WITH ROCK DRUMMING DVD VIDEO
Taught by the Legendary Former Guns N' Roses Drummer!
02501387 DVD......$29.99

AFRO-CARIBBEAN DRUM GROOVES
by Chuck Silverman
02500370 Book/CD Pack......$14.95

THE BOOK OF FUNK BEATS
Grooves for Snare, Bass, and Hi-hat
by David Lewitt
02500953 Book/CD Pack......$14.99

PONCHO SANCHEZ' CONGA COOKBOOK
by Poncho Sanchez with Chuck Silverman
02500278 Book/CD Pack......$16.95

DRUM EXERCISES FOR THE POP, FUNK, AND R&B PLAYER
by Ralph Johnson
02500827 Book/CD Pack......$14.99

DRUMMING THE EASY WAY!
The Beginner's Guide to Playing Drums for Students and Teachers
by Tom Hapke
02500876 Book/CD Pack......$19.95
02500191 Book Only......$12.95

DRUMMING THE EASY WAY! VOLUME 2
by Tom Hapke
02501060 Book/CD Pack......$17.95
02501064 Book Only......$12.95

LATIN FUNK CONNECTION DVD VIDEO
taught by Chuck Silverman
02501417 DVD......$24.99

BEST OF THE DAVE MATTHEWS BAND FOR DRUMS
02500184 Play-It-Like-It-Is Drum......$19.95

DAVE MATTHEWS BAND – FAN FAVORITES FOR DRUMS
02500643 Play-It-Like-It-Is Drum......$19.95

METALLICA – ...AND JUSTICE FOR ALL
02503504 Play-It-Like-It-Is Drum......$18.95

METALLICA – BLACK
02503509 Play-It-Like-It-Is Drum......$18.95

METALLICA: CLASSIC SONGS – DRUM LEGENDARY LICKS DVD VIDEO
taught by Jack E. Roth
A Step-By-Step Breakdown of Metallica's Drum Grooves and Fills
02500839 DVD......$24.95

METALLICA – DEATH MAGNETIC
02501315 Play-It-Like-It-Is Drum......$19.99

METALLICA – DRUM LEGENDARY LICKS
taught by Gregory Beyer
02500172 Book/CD Pack......$19.95

METALLICA – DRUM LEGENDARY LICKS 1983-1988 DVD VIDEO
A Step-by-Step Breakdown of Metallica's Drum Grooves and Fills
featuring Nathan Kilen
02500482 DVD......$24.95

METALLICA – DRUM LEGENDARY LICKS 1988-1997 DVD VIDEO
A Step-by-Step Breakdown of Metallica's Drum Grooves and Fills
featuring Nathan Kilen
02500485 DVD......$24.95

METALLICA – GARAGE INC.
02500077 Play-It-Like-It-Is Drum......$18.95

METALLICA – KILL 'EM ALL
02503508 Play-It-Like-It-Is Drum......$18.95

LEARN TO PLAY DRUMS WITH METALLICA
by Greg Beyer
02500190 Book/CD Pack......$14.95

LEARN TO PLAY DRUMS WITH METALLICA – VOLUME 2
by Dan Gross
02500887 Book/CD Pack......$15.95

METALLICA – MASTER OF PUPPETS
02503502 Play-It-Like-It-Is Drum......$18.95

METALLICA – RE-LOAD
02503517 Play-It-Like-It-Is Drum......$18.95

METALLICA – RIDE THE LIGHTNING
02503507 Play-It-Like-It-Is Drum......$17.95

METALLICA – ST. ANGER
02500640 Play-It-Like-It-Is Drum......$19.95

METALLICA'S LARS ULRICH
02506306 Book/CD Pack......$17.95

PONCHO SANCHEZ DVD VIDEO
Fundamentals of Latin Music for the Rhythm Section
featuring the Poncho Sanchez Latin Jazz Band
02500729 DVD......$24.95

1001 DRUM GROOVES
The Complete Resource for Every Drummer
by Steve Mansfield
02500337 Book......$12.95

66 DRUM SOLOS FOR THE MODERN DRUMMER
by Tom Hapke
02500319 Book/CD Pack......$16.95

RUSH – LEGENDARY LICKS FOR DRUMS DVD VIDEO
Taught and Performed by Jamie Borden
02500628 DVD......$24.95

See your local music retailer or contact:

cherry lane music company

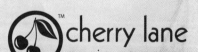

EXCLUSIVELY DISTRIBUTED BY
HAL•LEONARD CORPORATION
7777 W. Bluemound Rd. P.O. Box 13819 Milwaukee, WI 53213

Prices, contents, and availability subject to change without notice.

0909